Eye of the Times

PAUL CELAN
EYE OF THE TIMES

Selected, translated and introduced by
Jean Boase-Beier

Edited by Philip Wilson

2021

Published by Arc Publications,
Nanholme Mill, Shaw Wood Road
Todmorden OL14 6DA, UK
www.arcpublications.co.uk

Copyright in the poems ©
Translation copyright © Jean Boase-Beier, 2021
Introduction copyright © Jean Boase-Beier, 2021
Copyright in the present edition © Arc Publications 2021

978 1910345 04 7

Design by Tony Ward
Cover photograph by Tony Ward
Printed in the UK by Imprint Digital

ACKNOWLEDGEMENTS

'Todesfuge' and 'Der Reisekamerad' are from Paul Celan *Mohn und Gedächtnis*, © 1962 Deutsche Verlags-Anstalt, München, in der Verlagsgruppe Random House GmbH; 'Sprich auch Du', 'Auge der Zeit' and 'Argumentum e silentio' are from *Von Schweller zu Schweller*, © 1955 Deutsche Verlags-Anstalt, München, in der Verlagsgruppe Random House GmbH; 'Im Schlangenwagen, an', 'Stehen, im Schatten' and 'Ein Blatt, baumlos' are from Paul Celan, *Die Gedichte*. Kommentierte Gesamtausgabe in einem Band. Herausgegeben und kommentiert von Barbara Wiedemann, © 2003 Suhrkamp Verlag Frankfurt am Main; 'Erst wenn ich dich' and 'Wolfsbohne' are from Paul Celan, *Die Gedichte*. Neue kommentierte Gesamtausgabe. Mit 25 Radierungen von Gisèle Celan-Lestrange. Herausgegeben von Barbara Wiedemann, © 2018 Suhrkamp Verlag Berlin.

Arc Publications is grateful to the above named publishers for granting rights to reproduce these poems in the original German and in translation.

The translator, Jean Boase-Beier, would like to thank Philip Wilson for careful reading and pertinent questions and also Dieter Beier for helping prepare and check the manuscript.

This book is in copyright. Subject to statutory exception and to provision of relevant collective licensing agreements, no reproduction of any part of this book may take place without the written permission of Arc Publications.

  The translation of this work was supported by a grant from the Goethe-Institut

Arc Chapbook Series
Series Editor: Tony Ward

CONTENTS

Introduction / 7

12 / Todesfuge • Death Fugue / 13
16 / Der Reisekamerad • The Travelling Companion / 17
18 / Sprich auch Du • Speak, you too / 19
20 / Auge der Zeit • Eye of the Times / 21
22 / Argumentum e silentio • Argumentum e silentio / 23
26 / Wolfsbohne • Wolf's-Bean / 27
34 / Im Schlangenwagen, an • In the snake truck, and / 35
36 / Stehen, im Schatten • Standing, in the shadow / 37
38/ Ein Blatt, baumlos • A leaf, treeless / 39
40 / Erst wenn ich dich • Only when I touch / 41

Biographical Notes / 43

INTRODUCTION

"Absolutely not hermetic" (Ganz und gar nicht hermetisch) was how Paul Celan described his poetry in a phrase written in the front of one of his books, which he gave to his translator Michael Hamburger. Hamburger, perhaps more than any other translator, has come to be associated with Celan in English. He knew Celan personally, and experienced first hand how very sensitive the other poet could be: Celan mistakenly thought Hamburger had dared to call his poetry "hermetic".

Many other translators, most notably, perhaps, John Felstiner and Ian Fairley, have given us excellent versions of Celan. We might ask why we need another, but this would be the wrong question. It is more that poetry as complex as Celan's encourages and requires many different interpretations and translations, and each adds something to our understanding of the poet's work.

Born Paul Antschel in 1920 into a German-speaking Jewish family in the multilingual and multicultural city of Czernowitz, in Romania (now Chernivtsi in Ukraine), Celan went to France at age of 18, to begin studying Medicine in Tours. One year later the Second World War started and he returned home. Since Jews were not allowed to study sciences, he began studying French. At this time he started to write and translate poetry. In 1942, Celan was forced to work building roads, and his parents were taken to a concentration camp, where his father died and his mother was shot. When the war ended, Celan left Czernowitz, moving to Bucharest and publishing for the first time under the pseudonym Paul Celan, the name by which he would subsequently be known. In 1948 he moved to Paris, where he studied German and Linguistics, later becoming a university lecturer in German. He married the artist Gisèle de Lestrange in 1952, and they had two sons, François, who died soon after birth, and Eric. He became a French citizen in 1955.

From now on, his poetry was marked increasingly by his own personal trauma and that of the Jews more generally. He followed critical reception of his work closely, and was worried that his earliest poems might be thought to aestheticise suffering. His poetry, which is represented here in roughly chronological order, becomes sparer, less explicit, and more ambiguous, as time goes on. But, as several of his talks and writings indicate, his intention in using ambiguity was never to mystify, but always to communicate. The poems express complex feelings and situations, and each poem speaks differently to different readers.

Celan believed that both language and poetry could not help but be affected by the events of the previous years, events that were already becoming known by the early 1960s as the Holocaust. So he was sympathetic to the view that poetry should not be too explicit, but that it must incorporate the effects of trauma.

Celan's earlier poems are more open to immediate understanding, and his later poems are easier to understand in the context of the earlier ones. As Celan's views on poetry were developing, so also was his knowledge of what had happened to the Jews in the Holocaust. Working as a translator from the end of the war, he translated poetry and prose by Shakespeare, by the Russian writers Mandelstam, Lermontov and Chekhov, and by French writers such as Apollinaire, Cocteau, Simenon, and Rimbaud. He often gave public readings of his translations, as well as of his own poetry, especially in France and Germany. He received many poetry prizes in Germany.

In the mid-1960s he began to suffer more and more

from mental illness, and had to spend some time in hospital. Even at this time, he continued to read widely, to write poetry, and to translate. Traces of philosophers such as Martin Heidegger, Walter Benjamin, or Gershom Scholem are to be found everywhere in his poems, and the reader can hear echoes of many earlier poets: Gerard Manley Hopkins, Thomas Hardy, Rainer Maria Rilke, or Charles Baudelaire. And every poet he translated had an effect upon his work. When he was wrongly accused of plagiarising the poetry of Yvan Goll, which he had translated from French into German, Goll's widow, who made the accusation, in part used the perceived echoes of Goll's work in Celan's poems to mount a defamatory campaign, which caused Celan great distress.

His interest in botany, geology and medicine are also reflected in his poetry, as is his study of linguistics and especially his concern with etymology. For Celan, etymology was also semantics, in the sense that links between German words and words of other languages or from earlier stages of German still persist as part of the meaning of words used in everyday speech. For example, the German word for 'home' (Heim), which is found in the word for 'secret' (heimlich) is related not only to the Yiddish word for 'life' (khayim) but also, if one goes back to its assumed Proto-Indo-European roots, to the word *kei, 'to lie', which in German (liegen) gave the word 'Lager', a camp, and the word used in particular for a concentration camp. Connections of this sort are everywhere in Celan's work, and were for him a source of creativity, but also of fear or despair.

Celan also had an uneasy relationship with the Jewish faith of his parents, and indeed with religious thought in general; unable, like Hopkins, to embrace darkness along with light, he nevertheless knew that the two were inextricably linked. For Celan, this was an undeniable truth, but it was not a comfort. Living in separation from his family, suffering increasing mental distress, he committed suicide in 1970 by drowning himself in the Seine.

This small collection aims to give a picture of Celan's work; the note which accompanies each poem is not intended as an explanation, but simply as a brief contextual orientation for the reader, a starting-point for anyone who is not familiar with his poems.

Jean Boase-Beier

FURTHER READING

Fairley, I. (tr.) *Paul Celan: Fathomsuns and Benighted*, Manchester: Carcanet, 2001.

Fairley, I. (tr.) *Paul Celan: Snow Part and Other Poems* (1968-1969), Manchester: Carcanet, 2007.

Felstiner, J. *Paul Celan: Poet, Survivor, Jew,* New Haven and London: Yale University Press, 1995.

Felstiner, J. (tr.) *Selected Poems and Prose of Paul Celan*, New York and London: W. W. Norton, 2001.

Hamburger, M. (tr.) *Poems of Paul Celan,* 3rd edn, London: Anvil Press, 2007.

EYE OF THE TIMES

TODESFUGE

Schwarze Milch der Frühe wir trinken sie abends
wir trinken sie mittags und morgens wir trinken sie nachts
wir trinken und trinken
wir schaufeln ein Grab in den Lüften da liegt man nicht eng
Ein Mann wohnt im Haus der spielt mit den Schlangen der
    schreibt
der schreibt wenn es dunkelt nach Deutschland dein goldenes
    Haar Margarete
er schreibt es und tritt vor das Haus und es blitzen die Sterne
    er pfeift seine Rüden herbei
er pfeift seine Juden hervor läßt schaufeln ein Grab in der Erde
er befiehlt uns spielt auf nun zum Tanz

Schwarze Milch der Frühe wir trinken dich nachts
wir trinken dich morgens und mittags wir trinken dich abends
wir trinken und trinken
Ein Mann wohnt im Haus der spielt mit den Schlangen der
    schreibt
der schreibt wenn es dunkelt nach Deutschland dein goldenes
    Haar Margarete
Dein aschenes Haar Sulamith wir schaufeln ein Grab in den
    Lüften da liegt man nicht eng

DEATH FUGUE

Celan's most famous poem, written in the mid 1940s, appeared first in Petre Solomon's Romanian translation in 1947, then in German in 1952. Celan later rejected it, in part fearing criticism for aestheticising the concentration camps. Yet the poem is clearly ironical. There is a disturbing flippancy, but it is not the poet's: many different voices speak in the poem. There are echoes of Thomas Hardy, not only in the metre, but in the focus on voices.

Black milk of morning we drink it at evening
we drink it at noon and at dawn we drink it at night
we drink it and drink it
we shovel a grave in the air there you won't lie so tight
A man lives in the house he is playing with snakes and he writes
he writes when the dark comes to Germany your hair of gold Margarete
he writes it and steps from the house and the stars flash out and he whistles his pack to come here
he whistles his Jews to come out has them shovel a grave in the earth
he commands us play on for the dance

Black milk of morning we drink you at night
we drink you at dawn and at noon we drink you at dusk
we drink you and drink you
A man lives in the house he is playing with snakes and he writes
he writes when the dark comes to Germany your hair of gold Margarete
Your hair of ash Sulamith we shovel a grave in the air there you won't lie so tight

Er ruft stecht tiefer ins Erdreich ihr einen ihr andern singet
und spielt
er greift nach dem Eisen im Gurt er schwingts seine Augen
sind blau
stecht tiefer die Spaten ihr einen ihr andern spielt weiter zum
Tanz auf

Schwarze Milch der Frühe wir trinken dich nachts
wir trinken dich mittags und morgens wir trinken dich abends
wir trinken und trinken
Ein Mann wohnt im Haus dein goldenes Haar Margarete
dein aschenes Haar Sulamith er spielt mit den Schlangen

Er ruft spielt süßer den Tod der Tod ist ein Meister aus Deutschland
er ruft streicht dunkler die Geigen dann steigt ihr als Rauch in
die Luft
dann habt ihr ein Grab in den Wolken da liegt man nicht eng

Schwarze Milch der Frühe wir trinken dich nachts
wir trinken dich mittags der Tod ist ein Meister aus Deutschland
wir trinken dich abends und morgens wir trinken und trinken
der Tod ist ein Meister aus Deutschland sein Auge ist blau
er trifft dich mit bleierner Kugel er trifft dich genau
ein Mann wohnt im Haus dein goldenes Haar Margarete
er hetzt seine Rüden auf uns er schenkt uns ein Grab in der Luft
er spielt mit den Schlangen und träumet der Tod ist ein Meister aus
Deutschland
dein goldenes Haar Margarete
dein aschenes Haar Sulamith

He shouts cut the earth still deeper you lot you others sing up
    and play on
he grabs at the iron in his belt and he swings it his eyes are blue
cut deeper your spades you lot you others play on for the dance

Black milk of morning we drink you at night
we drink you at noon and at dawn we drink you at dusk
we drink you and drink you
a man lives in the house your hair of gold Margarete
your hair of ash Sulamith he is playing with snakes

He shouts play death still sweeter and death is a master from
    Germany
he shouts play your fiddles still darker then up you'll go as
    smoke in the air
and you'll have your grave in the clouds there you won't lie so tight

Black milk of morning we drink you at night
we drink you at noon and death is a master from Germany
we drink you at dusk and at dawn and we drink and we drink
and death is a master from Germany his eyes are blue
he hits you with bullets of lead and his aim is true
a man lives in the house your hair of gold Margarete
he sets his pack on us he gives us a grave in the air
he is playing with snakes and dreaming that death is a master
    from Germany
your hair of gold Margarete
your hair of ash Sulamith

DER REISEKAMERAD

Deiner Mutter Seele schwebt voraus.
Deiner Mutter Seele hilft die Nacht umschiffen, Riff um Riff.
Deiner Mutter Seele peitscht die Haie vor dir her.

Dieses Wort ist deiner Mutter Mündel.
Deiner Mutter Mündel teilt dein Lager, Stein um Stein.
Deiner Mutter Mündel bückt sich nach der Krume Lichts.

THE TRAVELLING COMPANION

> *Many of Celan's early poems focus on the memory of his mother, murdered in a concentration camp in 1942. The etymology of 'Mündel' (ward) suggests it initially meant someone who was protected, since the element '-mund' is related to 'Hand' (hand). Yet the word seems (and is often understood by German speakers) to mean someone for whom one speaks, because it appears to contain the root 'Mund' (mouth). Such folk etymologies held great fascination for Celan.*

The soul of your mother glides ahead.
The soul of your mother helps you navigate night, reef by reef.
The soul of your mother whips the sharks on before you.

This word is the ward of your mother.
The ward of your mother shares your quarters, stone by stone.
The ward of your mother bends for the crumb of light.

SPRICH AUCH DU

Sprich auch du,
sprich als letzter,
sag deinen Spruch.

Sprich –
Doch scheide das Nein nicht vom Ja.
Gib deinem Spruch auch den Sinn:
gib ihm den Schatten.

Gib ihm Schatten genug,
gib ihm so viel,
als du um dich verteilt weißt zwischen
Mittnacht und Mittag und Mittnacht.

Blicke umher:
sieh, wie's lebendig wird rings –
Beim Tode! Lebendig!
Wahr spricht, wer Schatten spricht.

Nun aber schrumpft der Ort, wo du stehst:
Wohin jetzt, Schattenentblößter, wohin?
Steige. Taste empor.
Dünner wirst du, unkenntlicher, feiner!
Feiner: ein Faden,
an dem er herabwill, der Stern:
um unten zu schwimmen, unten,
wo er sich schimmern sieht: in der Dünung
wandernder Worte.

SPEAK, YOU TOO

Questions of language form the basis for most of Celan's work. He asks how we can speak without using words that have lost meaning, or gained unwanted meaning, both in everyday usage and in poetry, by being aestheticized or made too black-and-white. As in English, the word 'Schatten' (shadow or shade) also suggests the dead.

Speak, you too,
speak as the last one,
say your say.

Speak –
But don't split the no from the yes
Give your say sense:
give it shadow.

Give it shadow enough,
give it as much
as you know to be strewn around you between
midnight and midday and midnight.

Glance about:
see how it grows alive all round -
In death! Alive!
To speak truth, speak shadow.

But it shrinks now, the place where you stand:
Where now, you whom shadow has bared, where to?
Go up. Grope upwards.
You'll grow thinner, unknowable, finer!
Finer: a thread
on which it wants to descend, the star:
to swim down below, below
where it sees itself shimmer: in the drift
of wandering words.

AUGE DER ZEIT

Dies ist das Auge der Zeit:
es blickt scheel
unter siebenfarbener Braue.
Sein Lid wird von Feuern gewaschen,
seine Träne ist Dampf.

Der blinde Stern fliegt es an
und zerschmilzt an der heißeren Wimper:
es wird warm in der Welt,
und die Toten
knospen und blühen.

EYE OF THE TIMES

Notable in this poem, from the early 1950s, is the use of Jewish symbols – fire, star, eye, the number seven – many of which became personal symbols for Celan. In his poems eyes suggest life, point of view and engagement, but often also the Jewish folk belief in the Evil Eye. And because, in German, dice have eyes rather than dots, eyes also suggest chance.

This is the eye of the times:
it looks out slant
under a seven-colour brow.
Its lid is bathed in flames,
its tear is steam.

The blind star flies at it
and melts on the hotter lash:
the world grows warm,
and the dead
break bud, and blossom.

ARGUMENTUM E SILENTIO

für René Char

An die Kette gelegt
zwischen Gold und Vergessen:
die Nacht.
Beide griffen nach ihr.
Beide ließ sie gewähren.

Lege,
lege auch du jetzt dorthin, was heraufdämmern
will neben den Tagen:
das sternüberflogene Wort,
das meerübergossne.

Jedem das Wort.
Jedem das Wort, das ihm sang,
als die Meute ihn hinterrücks anfiel –
Jedem das Wort, das ihm sang und erstarrte.

Ihr, der Nacht,
das sternüberflogne, das meerübergossne,
ihr das erschwiegne,
dem das Blut nicht gerann, als der Giftzahn
die Silben durchstieß.

Ihr das erschwiegene Wort.

ARGUMENTUM E SILENTIO

for René Char

An argument from silence is an argument that derives inferences from an absence, rather than from the presence of something. The golden chain in Judaism symbolises Jewish tradition, passed on from person to person and generation to generation. René Char is the French poet and resistance fighter whom Celan got to know in the 1950s, when he translated his poems into German.

Kept on a chain
between gold and forgetting:
night.
Both reached for her.
She let both have their way.

Lay down,
lay down there, you too, what wants
to dawn up with the days:
the word, starflown
sea-soaked.

To each their word.
To each the word that sang to them,
as the pack attacked from behind –
To each the word that sang to them and froze.

For her, for the night,
the starflown, the sea-soaked,
for her what silence achieved,
whose blood never froze when a poison fang
lanced through the syllables.

For her the word that silence achieved.

Wider die andern, die bald,
die umhurt von den Schinderohren,
auch Zeit und Zeiten erklimmen,
zeugt es zuletzt,
zuletzt, wenn nur Ketten erklingen,
zeugt es von ihr, die dort liegt
zwischen Gold und Vergessen,
beiden verschwistert von je –

Denn wo
dämmerts denn, sag, als bei ihr,
die im Stromgebiet ihrer Träne
tauchenden Sonnen die Saat zeigt
aber und abermals?

Against the others that soon, when,
whored round by cutthroats,
they too climb up time and times,
at last it bears witness
at the last, when only the chains ring out,
it bears witness for her, who lies there
between gold and forgetting,
sister to both from the start –

For where
does the dawn rise, say, but with her,
who holds up to suns, that wash in the riverforce
of her tears, this seed
time and time again?

WOLFSBOHNE

                              …o
Ihr Blüten von Deutschland, o mein Herz wird
Untrügbarer Kristall, an dem
Das Licht sich prüfet, wenn   Deutschland
                HÖLDERLIN, *Vom Abgrund nämlich...*

…wie an den Häusern der Juden (zum
Andenken des ruinierten Jerusalems), immer
etwas u n v o l l e n d e t gelassen werden muß…
                JEAN PAUL, *Das Kampaner Tal*

Leg den Riegel vor: Es
sind Rosen im Haus.
Es sind
sieben Rosen im Haus.
Unser
Kind
weiß es und schläft.

(Weit, in Michailowka, in
Gaissin, in
der Ukraine, wo
sie mir Vater und Mutter erschlugen: was
blühte dort, was
blüht dort? Welche
Blume, Mutter,
tat dir dort weh
mit ihrem Namen?

WOLF'S-BEAN

This poem was meant for inclusion in Celan's 1963 collection Die Niemandsrose *(The No-one Rose), but he took it out, perhaps from the same worry that led him to reject 'Death Fugue'. And yet it is one of his most powerful poems, full of grief and loss, an unbearable sense of loneliness, and an obsessive suspicion of the motives of others, a legacy of the traumatic events of his youth. He reworked the poem at least once, and the version given here includes his revisions.*

                              ... oh
You flowers of Germany, oh my heart becomes
Infallible crystal, on which
Light proves itself, if   Germany
                    HÖLDERLIN, *Vom Abgrund nämlich ...*

... as in the houses of Jews (as a
reminder of destroyed Jerusalem), something
must always be left i n c o m p l e t e.
                    JEAN PAUL, *Das Kampaner Tal*

Slide the bolt on: there
are roses in the house.
There are
seven roses in the house.
Our
child
knows this and sleeps.

(Far away, in Michailowka, in
Gaissin, in
Ukraine, where
they murdered Father and Mother: what
flowered there, what
flowers there? What
flower, mother,
hurt you there
with its name?

Mutter, dir
die du *Wolfsbohne* sagtest, nicht:
Lupine.

Gestern kam einer von ihnen und
tötete dich
zum andern Mal in
meinem Gedicht.

Mutter.

Mutter, wessen
Hand hab ich gedrückt,
da ich mit deinen
Worten ging nach
Deutschland?

In - -, sagtest du immer, in
- - an
der Elbe,
auf
der Flucht.
Mutter, es wohnten dort…

> Du, die du Wolfsbohne sagtest.
> Sie, die die Wolfsschanze bauten. – Wer
> lebt?
> Auf der Atemspur lebst du, auf
> Atemsuche, im
> Gedicht.

Mutter, ich habe
Briefe geschrieben.
Mutter, es kam keine Antwort.
Mutter, es kam eine Antwort.
Mutter, ich habe

You, Mother,
you who said *Wolfsbohne*, not:
lupin.

Yesterday
one of them came and
killed you
again in
my poem.

Mother.

Mother, whose hand did I shake
when I went with
your words to
Germany?

In - -, you always said, in
- - on
the Elbe,
in flight.
Mother, those who lived there were ...

> You, who said Wolf's-bean.
> They who built the Wolf's Lair. – Who
> is still alive?
> On the breath-trace you live, on
> the breath-search, in
> poems.

Mother, I have
written letters.
Mother, no answer came.
Mother, an answer came.
Mother, I have

Briefe geschrieben an –
Mutter, sie schreiben Gedichte.
Mutter, sie schrieben sie nicht,
wär das Gedicht nicht, das
ich geschrieben hab um
deinet-
willen, um
deines
Gottes
willen.
Gelobt, sprachst du, sei
der Ewige und
gepriesen, drei-
mal
Amen.

Mutter, sie schweigen.
Mutter, sie dulden es, daß
die Niedertracht uns verleumdet.
Mutter, keiner
fällt den Mördern ins Wort.

Mutter, sie schreiben Gedichte.
O
Mutter, wieviel
fremdester Acker trägt deine Frucht!
Trägt sie und nährt
die da töten!

Mutter, ich
bin verloren.
Mutter, wir
sind verloren.
Mutter, mein Kind, das
dir ähnlich sieht.)

written letters to –
Mother, they write poems.
Mother, they would not write
but for the poem I
have written, for
your sake, for
your
God's
sake.
Praised, you said, be
the Eternal and
lauded three
times
Amen.

Mother, they are silent.
Mother, they allow it,
that vileness slanders us.
Mother, no-one
cuts off the murderers' words.

Mother, they write poems.
Oh
Mother, how many
foreignest fields bear your fruit!
Bear it and
feed those that kill!

Mother, I
am lost.
Mother, we
are lost.
Mother, my child,
who looks like you.)

Leg den Riegel vor: Es
sind Rosen im Haus.
Es sind
sieben Rosen im Haus.
Es ist
der Siebenleuchter im Haus.
Unser
Kind
weiß es und schläft.

Mutter, Unverlorene, mit uns,
den Unverlorenen,
siegst du.
Und mit uns Wahr und Gerecht und Gerade,
um
der versöhnenden
Liebe
willen.

Slide the bolt on: there
are roses in the house.
There are
seven roses in the house.
There is
the seven-branched candelabrum in the house.
Our
child
knows this and sleeps.

Mother, unlost, with us,
the unlost,
you triumph.
And with us, the true, the just, the upright,
for
peace-bringing
love's
sake.

'IM SCHLANGENWAGEN, AN...'

Im Schlangenwagen, an
der weißen Zypresse vorbei,
durch die Flut
fuhren sie dich.

Doch in dir, von
Geburt,
schäumte die andre Quelle,
am schwarzen
Strahl Gedächtnis
klommst du zutag.

'IN THE SNAKE TRUCK, AND...'

> *This poem, published in 1967, is typical of the obliqueness with which Celan, especially in later poems, describes what appears to be a memory, or a poetic reconstruction, of the events of the 1940s.*

In the snake truck, and
past the white cypress,
through the flood
they drove you.

But in you, from
birth,
foamed that other source,
on the black
ray memory
you climbed up to daylight.

'STEHEN, IM SCHATTEN...'

Stehen, im Schatten
des Wundenmals in der Luft.

Für-niemand-und-nichts-Stehn.
Unerkannt,
für dich
allein.

Mit allem, was darin Raum hat,
auch ohne
Sprache.

'STANDING, IN THE SHADOW...'

> *Celan uses many words in his poems for wounds, scars and injuries. They reflect trauma, and the after-effects of trauma upon language, and even upon silence.*

Standing, in the shadow
of the woundmark in the air.

Standing-for-no-one-and-nothing.
Unrecognised,
for yourself
alone.

With all there's room for
if need be without
language.

'EIN BLATT, BAUMLOS...'

Ein Blatt, baumlos
für Bertolt Brecht:

Was sind das für Zeiten,
wo ein Gespräch
beinah ein Verbrechen ist,
weil es soviel Gesagtes
mit einschließt?

'A LEAF, TREELESS...'

Here Celan makes reference to Bertolt Brecht's 1939 poem 'An die Nachgeborenen' (To Those who Come After). In that poem, Brecht questions the possibility of talking about trees when that means to be silent about the horrors that had already begun. Thirty years later Celan asks how we can talk at all without using language already tainted by earlier use.

A leaf, treeless
for Bertolt Brecht:

What times are these
when conversation
is almost a crime
because so much said
before is in it?

'ERST WENN ICH DICH...'

Erst wenn ich dich
als Schatten berühre,
glaubst du mir meinen
Mund,

der klettert mit Spät-
sinnigem droben
in Zeithöfen
umher,

du stößt zur Heerschar
der Zweitverwerter unter
den Engeln,

Schweigewütiges
sternt.

'ONLY WHEN I TOUCH...'

> *A late poem that appeared after Celan's death. It is of the type that caused people to view the poet as hermetic. It is left to the reader to work out the identity of the 'you' from whom the speaker hopes for both recognition and communion after death. As noted in 'The Travelling Companion', the element '-mund', when in words for protection or authority, relates to 'Hand' (hand). The word 'Mund' (mouth) in this poem is not related to 'Hand'; nevertheless, Celan often made a connection between the speaking mouth and the hand that communicates by writing or shaking the hand of another. It is probably this connection that allows him to follow 'mouth' with 'clambers'.*

Only when I touch you
as a shadow
will you believe in
my mouth,

it clambers around with
the latesensical
in time-courts
back there,

you press on to the
host of re-users
among the angels,

the silent-angry
will star.

BIOGRAPHICAL NOTES

PAUL CELAN, who was born Paul Antschel, is widely considered to be one of the foremost European poets of the twentieth century. Born in 1920 into a German-speaking Jewish family in Czernowitz, at that time a multicultural city in Romania, he spent a short time studying Medicine in France before the start of the Second World War forced him to return. Back in Czernowitz, he began to write and translate poems, while studying French and Russian, but persecution of the Jews led to the deportation of his parents to a concentration camp, where his father died and his mother was shot. This sudden loss was to lead to severe trauma from which Celan never recovered. After the war he went to Paris, where he worked as a university lecturer in German, and won many awards for his poetry. In spite of his success, he was increasingly troubled by uncertainty, lack of self-belief, and mental disturbance. He drowned himself in the Seine in 1970.

JEAN BOASE-BEIER, who is Arc Publications' Translations Editor, is a translator of German poetry and an academic writer. She is Professor Emerita of Literature and Translation at the University of East Anglia, where she founded the MA in Literary Translation in 1992 and ran it until 2015.

Her academic work focuses on translation, style and poetry, and especially on the translation of Holocaust poetry. Academic publications include *Translating the Poetry of the Holocaust* (2015, Bloomsbury), the co-edited *Palgrave Handbook of Literary Translation* (2018), and *Translation and Style* (2020, Routledge).

Her poetry translations (all from Arc Publications) include collections by modern German poets Ernst Meister (2003), Rose Ausländer (2014), and Volker von Törne (2017), and she has recently co-edited (with Marian de Vooght) *Poetry of the Holocaust: An Anthology* (2019).